Love Beyond Words: Exploring the Five Languages. Understanding, Embracing, and Celebrating Love

DNT Publishing

Published by DNT Publishing, 2024.

While every precaution has been taken in the preparation of this book, the publisher assumes no responsibility for errors or omissions, or for damages resulting from the use of the information contained herein.

LOVE BEYOND WORDS: EXPLORING THE FIVE LANGUAGES. UNDERSTANDING, EMBRACING, AND CELEBRATING LOVE

First edition. February 11, 2024.

Copyright © 2024 DNT Publishing.

ISBN: 979-8224658541

Written by DNT Publishing.

Table of Contents

Introduction

Love is a complex and multifaceted emotion that plays a central role in our lives. In the realm of relationships, understanding how individuals express and receive love is crucial for fostering deep connections. This textbook delves into the concept of love languages, a framework that illuminates the diverse ways people communicate and experience love.

1.1 Defining Love Languages

In this section, we will provide a comprehensive definition of love languages, exploring the origins of the concept and its relevance in modern relationships. By establishing a solid foundation, readers will gain a clear understanding of the significance of love languages.

1.2 Importance of Love Languages in Relationships

Building upon the definition, we will delve into why love languages are essential for healthy and fulfilling relationships. This section will highlight the impact of understanding and embracing love languages on communication, intimacy, and overall relationship satisfaction.

1.1 Defining Love Languages

Love languages refer to the distinct and personalized ways individuals express and perceive love. Coined by Dr. Gary Chapman, this concept asserts that people have unique preferences in how they receive affection, and recognizing and understanding these preferences is key to building successful relationships.

In this section, we will explore the five primary love languages identified by Dr. Chapman:

1. Words of Affirmation:
- Examining the power of verbal expressions of love.
- Understanding how affirming words impact emotional well-being.
- Communication strategies for effectively expressing words of affirmation.

2. Acts of Service:
- Investigating the role of actions in conveying love.
- Analyzing the significance of acts of service in relationships.
- Practical tips for incorporating acts of service into daily life.

3. Receiving Gifts:
- Exploring the symbolism and emotional value of gift-giving.
- Understanding how gifts serve as expressions of love.
- Guidance on selecting meaningful and thoughtful gifts.

4. Quality Time:
- Defining the importance of undivided attention in relationships.
- Strategies for creating quality time amidst busy lifestyles.

- Recognizing the impact of shared experiences on emotional connections.

5. Physical Touch:

- Examining the role of physical contact in conveying love.
- Differentiating between various forms of physical touch.
- Addressing the significance of intimacy and affectionate touch.

1.2 Importance of Love Languages in Relationships

Understanding and acknowledging love languages are pivotal factors in nurturing healthy and fulfilling relationships. This section will delve into the significance of love languages and their impact on various aspects of relationship dynamics.

Enhancing Communication:

- Exploring how awareness of love languages facilitates effective communication.
- Addressing potential miscommunications and conflicts arising from differing love languages.
- Strategies for fostering open and honest dialogue about individual preferences.

Building Emotional Intimacy:

- Recognizing the role of love languages in deepening emotional connections.
- Exploring how expressing love in a partner's preferred language fosters intimacy.
- Case studies illustrating the positive effects of aligning love languages.

Increasing Relationship Satisfaction:

- Examining research on the correlation between love languages and relationship satisfaction.
- Strategies for adapting behaviors to meet the emotional needs of partners.
- Creating a love language-centric environment to enhance overall relationship happiness.

Navigating Challenges:

- Addressing common challenges in relationships related to love language differences.
- Providing practical advice for overcoming obstacles and maintaining harmony.
- Emphasizing the adaptive nature of love languages throughout a relationship.

Personal Growth and Reflection:

• Encouraging individuals to reflect on their own love languages for personal growth.

• Exploring how self-awareness contributes to stronger interpersonal connections.

• Recognizing the evolving nature of love languages and the importance of ongoing reflection.

2. The Five Love Languages

This section will comprehensively explore the five distinct love languages identified by Dr. Gary Chapman. Each subsection will delve into the unique characteristics of a particular love language, providing insights into how individuals express and receive love.

2.1 Words of Affirmation:

• Understanding the power of verbal expressions in conveying love.

• Exploring the impact of positive affirmations on emotional well-being.

• Practical tips for effectively communicating words of affirmation to a partner.

2.2 Acts of Service:

• Examining the significance of actions as a love language.

• Analyzing how acts of service contribute to relationship satisfaction.

• Guidance on incorporating meaningful acts of service into daily life.

2.3 Receiving Gifts:

• Exploring the emotional symbolism of gift-giving in relationships.

• Understanding the role of thoughtful gifts as expressions of love.

• Tips for selecting and presenting gifts that resonate with a partner's preferences.

2.4 Quality Time:

• Defining the importance of undivided attention in building connections.

• Strategies for creating quality time amidst busy schedules.

• Recognizing shared experiences as crucial for fulfilling relationships.

2.5 Physical Touch:

- Examining the role of physical contact in conveying love and affection.
- Differentiating between various forms of physical touch.
- Addressing the significance of intimacy and tactile expressions of love.

2.1 Words of Affirmation

serve as a powerful love language, where verbal expressions play a central role in conveying love and appreciation. In this section, we will delve into the intricacies of this love language, exploring its impact on relationships and providing guidance on effective communication.

Understanding the Power of Verbal Expressions:

• Examining how words can shape emotions and strengthen bonds.

• Exploring the psychological impact of positive affirmations on individuals.

The Impact of Positive Affirmations on Emotional Well-being:

• Investigating how words of affirmation contribute to mental and emotional health.

• Recognizing the role of encouragement in building self-esteem and confidence.

Practical Tips for Effectively Communicating Words of Affirmation:

• Providing actionable strategies for expressing love through words.

• Offering guidance on crafting sincere and meaningful affirmations.

• Addressing challenges and common misconceptions in communicating verbally.

Case Studies:

• Real-life examples illustrate the positive effects of words of affirmation in relationships.

• Examining how couples navigate challenges through effective verbal communication.

Understanding Words of Affirmation

Words of affirmation represent a love language where verbal expressions play a significant role in communicating love, support, and appreciation. In this section, we will explore the nuances of understanding and utilizing words of affirmation in relationships.

The Essence of Verbal Communication:

• Highlighting the importance of verbal expressions in human connection.

• Exploring how spoken words can convey emotions and strengthen relational bonds.

Types of Words of Affirmation:

• Identifying different forms of affirmations, including compliments, encouragement, and expressions of love.

• Understanding the diversity of verbal communication styles within the words of affirmation love language.

Impact on Emotional Well-being:

• Examining the psychological and emotional effects of positive affirmations.

• Discuss how affirming words contribute to an individual's sense of self-worth and happiness.

Effective Communication Strategies:

• Providing practical tips for effectively expressing words of affirmation.

• Addressing the importance of sincerity and authenticity in verbal expressions of love.

• Offering guidance on adapting communication styles to align with a partner's preferences.

Navigating Challenges:

• Acknowledging potential challenges in communicating through words of affirmation.

• Offering strategies for overcoming obstacles and fostering a supportive verbal environment.

• Encouraging open communication about preferences and expectations related to affirmations.

Effective Communication through Words

When words serve as a primary means of expressing love, mastering the art of effective communication becomes crucial. In this section, we will explore strategies for communicating love through words of affirmation in a manner that resonates deeply with your partner.

Clear and Specific Expressions:

- Emphasizing the importance of clarity and specificity in verbal affirmations.
- Providing examples of how precise language enhances the impact of affirmations.

Timing and Frequency:

- Discussing the significance of timing in delivering affirming words.
- Exploring the balance between spontaneity and intentional affirmation.
- Guidance on establishing a consistent and supportive verbal communication routine.

Tailoring Affirmations to Your Partner:

- Recognizing individual preferences and tailoring affirmations accordingly.
- Strategies for discovering your partner's preferred language within words of affirmation.
- Creating a personalized repertoire of affirming expressions based on your partner's unique qualities.

Authenticity and Sincerity:

- Stressing the importance of authenticity in verbal expressions of love.
- Offering tips on conveying sincerity to ensure the genuine impact of affirmations.
- Addressing common pitfalls and misconceptions related to authenticity.

Receiving and Processing Feedback:

- Encouraging open communication about how affirmations are received.
- Strategies for actively listening to your partner's verbal needs and adjusting communication accordingly.
- Navigating constructive feedback to improve and refine verbal expressions of love.

2.2 Acts of Service

Acts of service represent a love language characterized by meaningful actions that demonstrate love and care. In this section, we will explore the intricacies of acts of service as a way of expressing and receiving love within relationships.

Examining the Significance of Actions:

- Understanding how actions can speak louder than words in conveying love.
- Exploring the emotional impact of thoughtful gestures and helpful deeds.

Contributions to Relationship Satisfaction:

- Analyzing how acts of service contribute to overall relationship satisfaction.
- Recognizing the role of these actions in building a sense of security and support.

Guidance on Incorporating Acts of Service:

- Providing practical tips for incorporating meaningful acts of service into daily life.
- Discussing the importance of intentionality and genuine effort in service-oriented gestures.

Balancing Acts of Service with Other Love Languages:

- Recognizing the need for a balanced approach to expressing love.
- Exploring how acts of service can complement other love languages within a relationship.

Case Studies:

- Real-life examples illustrating the positive effects of acts of service in relationships.
- Examining how couples navigate challenges and strengthen their bonds through meaningful actions.

Exploring Acts of Service as a Love Language

Acts of service constitute a unique love language where meaningful actions and deeds take center stage in expressing love. In this section, we will delve into the intricacies of exploring acts of service as a primary means of communicating and receiving love within relationships.

Understanding the Significance of Actions:

• Unpacking how actions can convey love and care more tangibly than words.

• Exploring the emotional impact of thoughtful gestures and helpful deeds in relationships.

The Role of Acts of Service in Relationship Dynamics:

• Analyzing how acts of service contribute to building a strong foundation in relationships.

• Recognizing how these actions can foster a sense of security and mutual support.

Practical Tips for Meaningful Gestures:

• Providing actionable advice on incorporating acts of service into daily life.

• Discussing the importance of genuine effort and intentionality in service-oriented actions.

• Offering creative ideas for acts of service that resonate with a partner's preferences.

Aligning Acts of Service with Partner Preferences:

• Recognizing the diversity of preferences within acts of service.

• Strategies for understanding and aligning service-oriented gestures with a partner's unique needs and desires.

Harmonizing Acts of Service with Other Love Languages:

• Exploring how acts of service can complement and enhance other love languages.

• Discuss the importance of a balanced approach to expressing love within the context of a relationship.

Nurturing Relationships through Actions

Acts of service play a vital role in nurturing relationships by translating love into tangible and thoughtful deeds. In this section, we will explore how intentional actions can contribute to the growth and well-being of a relationship.

Creating a Culture of Support:

• Examining how acts of service foster a supportive environment within a relationship.

• Discussing the impact of feeling supported through meaningful actions.

Expressing Love Through Deeds:

• Understanding how actions become a language of love in everyday life.

• Exploring the emotional resonance of deeds that demonstrate care and consideration.

Building Trust and Reliability:

• Analyzing how consistent acts of service contribute to building trust.

• Recognizing the role of reliability in creating a strong foundation for the relationship.

Practical Acts of Service for Relationship Nurturing:

• Providing a repertoire of practical and meaningful acts of service.

• Offering suggestions for adapting actions to various relationship contexts and stages.

Communication through Actions:

• Discuss how acts of service serve as a form of non-verbal communication.

• Highlighting the importance of understanding the intentions behind each action.

Case Studies:

• Real-life examples illustrating how couples nurture their relationships through intentional acts of service.

• Examining the positive impact of these actions on the overall well-being of the relationship.

2.3 Receiving Gifts

Receiving gifts is a love language where thoughtful and meaningful presents become expressions of love and care. In this section, we will explore the dynamics of this love language, understanding the significance of gift-giving in relationships.

Emotional Symbolism of Gift-Giving:

- Exploring how gifts serve as emotional symbols of love and appreciation.
- Understanding the psychological impact of receiving thoughtful presents.

Expressions of Love through Thoughtful Gifts:

- Analyzing how the selection and presentation of gifts communicate love.
- Recognizing the importance of personalization in gift-giving.

Selecting Meaningful and Thoughtful Gifts:

- Guiding choosing gifts that resonate with a partner's preferences.
- Discussing the significance of considering the recipient's interests and desires.

Celebrating Special Occasions:

- Exploring how gift-giving enhances celebrations and special moments.
- Strategies for aligning gifts with the significance of specific occasions.

Balancing Extrinsic and Intrinsic Value:

- Discussing the balance between the material and emotional aspects of gift-giving.
- Understanding that the thought and effort behind a gift often hold greater importance.

Case Studies:

- Real-life examples illustrating the positive impact of thoughtful gift-giving in relationships.
- Examining how couples navigate challenges and strengthen their connections through the exchange of meaningful gifts.

Unwrapping the Significance of Gift-Giving

Gift-giving as a love language involves more than the exchange of physical items—it is a nuanced expression of love and thoughtfulness. In this section, we will delve into the layers of significance behind gift-giving within the context of relationships.

Symbolism and Emotional Depth:

- Exploring how gifts symbolize love, appreciation, and thoughtfulness.
- Understanding the emotional depth that well-chosen presents can convey.

Personalization and Connection:

- Discussing the importance of personalizing gifts to reflect the recipient's preferences.
- Exploring how tailored gifts strengthen the sense of connection between individuals.

Communication through Gifts:

- Analyzing how gifts serve as a form of non-verbal communication.
- Discuss the messages and emotions conveyed through the act of giving and receiving gifts.

Occasions and Spontaneity:

- Recognizing the role of gifts in celebrating special occasions.
- Highlighting the impact of spontaneous and unexpected gifts on relationship dynamics.

Appreciation and Gratitude:

- Discuss how the act of giving gifts fosters an environment of appreciation.
- Exploring the reciprocal nature of expressing gratitude for received gifts.

Cultural and Personal Influences:

- Recognizing how cultural and individual factors influence the significance of gift-giving.
- Discussing the diverse ways in which people perceive and value presents.

Expressing Love through Thoughtful Gifts

Within the love language of receiving gifts, the act of giving becomes a profound expression of love and consideration. In this section, we will explore the art of expressing love through the selection and presentation of thoughtful gifts.

The Emotional Resonance of Gifts:

• Delving into how gifts carry emotional significance beyond their material value.

• Understanding how the thought behind a gift amplifies its impact.

Choosing Gifts with Intention:

• Guiding selecting gifts that resonate with a partner's preferences and interests.

• Discussing the importance of considering the recipient's personality and desires.

Personalization and Meaning:

• Exploring how personalization adds depth and meaning to gifts.

• Discuss creative ways to tailor gifts to reflect the unique qualities of the recipient.

Celebrating Love through Special Gifts:

• Highlighting the role of special occasions in enhancing the meaning of gifts.

• Strategies for choosing gifts that align with the significance of specific moments in the relationship.

Surprising with Thoughtful Gestures:

• Discussing the impact of surprise gifts and spontaneous acts of generosity.

• Recognizing how unexpected gestures contribute to the overall joy of receiving gifts.

Case Studies:

• Real-life examples illustrating how individuals express love through carefully chosen and thoughtful gifts.

• Examining the positive impact of these expressions on the emotional connection within relationships.

2.4 Quality Time

Quality time is a love language that emphasizes the importance of undivided attention and shared experiences in building and nurturing relationships. In this section, we will explore the nuances of quality time as a means of expressing and receiving love.

Defining the Essence of Quality Time:

- Unpacking the significance of focused and undivided attention in relationships.
- Understanding how quality time contributes to emotional connection.

Strategies for Creating Quality Time:

- Providing practical tips for carving out meaningful moments in daily life.
- Discussing the importance of intentionality in spending quality time together.

Recognizing Shared Experiences:

- Exploring how shared activities and experiences strengthen relational bonds.
- Understanding the impact of creating lasting memories through quality time.

Balancing Presence and Activities:

- Discussing the balance between being present in the moment and engaging in shared activities.
- Recognizing the importance of genuine connection during quality time.

Quality Time in Different Relationship Settings:

- Examining how quality time manifests in various relationship contexts, such as friendships and family dynamics.
- Strategies for adapting quality time practices to different relationship types.

The Essence of Quality Time in Relationships

Quality time, as a love language, revolves around the profound connection created through focused and meaningful shared experiences. In this section, we will explore the core essence of quality time in relationships.

Undivided Attention:

• Understanding the significance of giving undivided attention to a partner.

• Exploring how focused attention fosters a deeper emotional connection.

Emotional Presence:

• Discussing the importance of being emotionally present during shared moments.

• Recognizing how genuine engagement enhances the quality of time spent together.

Creating Meaningful Moments:

• Unpacking the idea that quality time is about more than quantity.

• Highlighting the impact of creating and cherishing meaningful moments together.

Building a Shared History:

• Exploring how shared experiences contribute to the narrative of a relationship.

• Discussing the role of shared memories in strengthening the bond between individuals.

Intentionality in Time Spent Together:

• Emphasizing the value of intentional planning and prioritization of quality time.

• Providing strategies for making the most of the time spent together.

Quality Time as a Form of Emotional Investment:

• Recognizing the act of dedicating time as a significant emotional investment in a relationship.

• Discussing the reciprocal nature of giving and receiving through quality time.

Building Connections through Time Spent Together

Quality time serves as a powerful tool for building and strengthening connections within relationships. In this section, we will explore how intentional time spent together contributes to the growth and depth of connections between individuals.

Shared Experiences as Building Blocks:

• Understanding how shared activities and experiences form the foundation of a connection.

• Exploring the role of common interests in creating a sense of unity.

Deepening Emotional Bonds:

• Examining how quality time contributes to emotional intimacy.

• Discussing the vulnerability and openness that arise during shared moments.

Communication Beyond Words:

• Recognizing that quality time is a form of non-verbal communication.

• Exploring the nuances of understanding each other through actions and presence.

Creating Lasting Memories:

• Discussing the impact of creating and cherishing memories together.

• Exploring how shared experiences contribute to the narrative of a relationship.

Quality Time as a Priority:

• Emphasizing the importance of making time spent together a conscious priority.

• Strategies for navigating busy schedules and incorporating quality time into daily life.

Adapting to Change and Growth:

• Recognizing the evolving nature of connections through shared experiences.

• Strategies for adapting quality time practices to accommodate changes in relationships over time.

2.5 Physical Touch

Physical touch is a love language that emphasizes the significance of tactile expressions in conveying love and affection. In this section, we will explore the dynamics of physical touch as a means of expressing and receiving love within relationships.

The Power of Physical Contact:

• Examining how physical touch serves as a powerful conduit for emotional connection.

• Understanding the physiological and psychological effects of touch.

Different Forms of Physical Touch:

• Exploring the diverse ways individuals may express and receive physical affection.

• Recognizing the importance of understanding and respecting personal boundaries.

Enhancing Intimacy through Touch:

• Discussing how physical touch contributes to the overall intimacy of a relationship.

• Strategies for deepening emotional bonds through affectionate touch.

Communication through Body Language:

• Analyzing how physical touch serves as a form of non-verbal communication.

• Discussing the messages conveyed through various forms of touch.

Balancing Comfort and Sensuality:

• Recognizing the balance between providing comfort through touch and expressing sensuality.

• Strategies for navigating differences in preferences and comfort levels.

Physical Touch Across Different Relationship Types:

• Examining how physical touch manifests in various relationships, including romantic partnerships, friendships, and familial connections.

• Strategies for expressing appropriate and meaningful touch in different contexts.

The Power of Physical Touch as a Love Language

Physical touch serves as a potent love language, encompassing a range of tactile expressions that communicate deep emotions and foster connection within relationships. In this section, we will explore the profound impact and significance of physical touch as a means of expressing and receiving love.

Emotional Connection through Touch:

• Examining how physical touch creates a unique and powerful emotional connection.

• Understanding the role of touch in conveying love, comfort, and security.

Physiological and Psychological Effects:

• Exploring the physiological and psychological benefits of positive physical touch.

• Discussing the release of oxytocin and the impact on stress reduction and emotional well-being.

Forms of Expressing Affection:

• Recognizing the diversity of ways individuals express affection through touch.

• Understanding the importance of mutual understanding and consent in physical interactions.

Fostering Intimacy:

• Discussing how physical touch contributes to the overall intimacy of a relationship.

• Exploring the role of touch in deepening emotional bonds and creating a sense of closeness.

Non-Verbal Communication:

• Analyzing how physical touch serves as a powerful form of non-verbal communication.

• Discussing the nuances of understanding and responding to the messages conveyed through touch.

Healing and Comfort:

• Recognizing the comforting and healing aspects of physical touch during times of distress.

• Exploring how touch provides a sense of reassurance and support.

Enhancing Intimacy through Touch

Physical touch is a powerful tool for deepening emotional bonds and enhancing intimacy within relationships. In this section, we will explore how intentional and affectionate touch contributes to creating a strong sense of closeness and connection.

The Intimacy of Affectionate Touch:

● Examining how affectionate touch fosters a unique form of emotional intimacy.

● Understanding the role of physical closeness in building a deeper connection.

Navigating Different Forms of Touch:

● Recognizing the diversity of touch and its varying levels of intimacy.

● Strategies for navigating and understanding personal preferences and boundaries.

Creating Rituals of Affection:

● Discussing the importance of establishing rituals or routines involving touch.

● Exploring how consistent physical affection contributes to a sense of security.

Expressing Love and Vulnerability:

● Analyzing how touch becomes a means of expressing love, vulnerability, and trust.

● Discussing the reciprocal nature of sharing and receiving affection through touch.

Communication Beyond Words:

● Recognizing how touch serves as a non-verbal form of communication in relationships.

● Discussing the emotional messages conveyed through different forms of physical contact.

Building a Physical Connection:

● Strategies for intentionally building a physical connection with a partner.

- Understanding the role of open communication in aligning touch preferences.

3. Identifying Your Love Language

Discovering and understanding your love language is a crucial step in building healthier and more fulfilling relationships. In this section, we will explore effective methods for identifying your primary love language.

Self-Reflection Exercises:

- Providing guided self-reflection exercises to help individuals uncover their preferred ways of giving and receiving love.

- Exploring personal experiences and emotions related to different love languages.

Communication with Your Partner:

- Discussing the importance of open communication with a partner to understand each other's love languages.

- Strategies for initiating conversations about love languages within a relationship.

Recognizing Love Languages in Others:

- Offering insights into how to observe and identify the love languages of friends, family, and partners.

- Discussing the benefits of recognizing and respecting diverse love languages in different relationships.

Online Love Language Assessments:

- Introducing online tools and assessments designed to help individuals identify their love languages.

- Providing information on reputable resources for taking love language quizzes.

Common Signs and Preferences:

- Highlighting common signs that may indicate a person's primary love language.

- Discuss how personal preferences in expressions of love can provide valuable clues.

Journaling and Reflection:

• Encouraging individuals to maintain a journal to track and reflect on experiences related to different love languages.

• Providing prompts for journaling about moments of connection and emotional fulfillment.

Self-Reflection Exercises for Identifying Your Love Language

Embarking on a journey of self-discovery is essential for understanding your love language. Engage in the following self-reflection exercises to uncover patterns, preferences, and emotional responses that may reveal your primary love language:

Recall Meaningful Moments:

- Reflect on past experiences in relationships. Identify moments that brought you immense joy, contentment, or fulfillment.

- Consider the actions or gestures that resonated with you most during these occasions.

Explore Childhood Influences:

- Delve into your childhood experiences and relationships. Recall how your caregivers expressed love and affection.

- Note any specific behaviors or expressions that made you feel loved and secure.

Examine Emotional Responses:

- Pay attention to your emotional responses in different situations. Identify activities or gestures that evoke a strong positive emotional reaction.

- Take note of instances where you felt deeply connected or appreciated.

Consider Unfulfilled Needs:

- Reflect on any unmet needs or desires in your current relationships. Consider the ways in which you feel most loved and supported.

• Identify aspects that, when lacking, may lead to feelings of discontent or emotional distance.

Analyze Communication Preferences:

• Explore your communication style and preferences. Consider whether you express love more through words, actions, gifts, quality time, or physical touch.

• Reflect on how you feel most valued when receiving love from others.

Complete a Love Language Quiz:

• Take advantage of online love language quizzes, such as those based on the work of Dr. Gary Chapman.

• Answer questions honestly to receive insights into your primary and secondary love languages.

Journaling Exercise:

• Start a journal dedicated to your experiences with love and relationships.

• Regularly jot down moments of connection, expressions of love, and reflections on how they made you feel.

Communication with Your Partner about Love Languages

Effective communication with your partner is essential for understanding each other's love languages and building a stronger connection. Follow these strategies to initiate conversations about love languages:

Choose a Comfortable Setting:

- Select a time and place where both you and your partner can have an open and relaxed conversation.

- Ensure that you have privacy and minimal distractions to focus on the discussion.

Express Your Intention:

- communicate your intention to strengthen the relationship by understanding each other's love languages.

- Emphasize the positive impact it can have on enhancing emotional connection.

Share Your Insights:

- Begin by sharing your reflections on your love language. Discuss moments or actions that make you feel loved and valued.

- Use specific examples to illustrate your preferences.

Encourage Your Partner to Share:

- Create a safe space for your partner to express their thoughts and feelings about love languages.

- Encourage them to share experiences and examples that highlight their preferred ways of giving and receiving love.

Use "I" Statements:

- Frame your statements using "I" to express your own feelings and experiences rather than placing blame or making assumptions.

- For example, say, "I feel loved when..." or "I appreciate it when..."

Ask Open-Ended Questions:

- Pose open-ended questions to facilitate a deeper discussion. Examples include:

- "Can you share a moment when you felt particularly loved?"

- "What gestures or actions make you feel most appreciated?"

Be an Active Listener:

- Practice active listening by giving your partner your full attention.

- Demonstrate empathy and understanding by paraphrasing what your partner shares and asking follow-up questions.

Jointly Explore Love Languages:

- Consider exploring love languages together. Take an online quiz or read literature on the topic.

- Discuss the results and how they resonate with your own experiences and preferences.

Be Open to Adjustment:

- Acknowledge that love languages can evolve over time or in different circumstances.

- Be open to adjusting your expressions of love based on your partner's evolving needs.

Express Gratitude:

• Express gratitude for your partner's willingness to engage in the conversation.

• Reinforce the idea that understanding and embracing each other's love languages can lead to a more fulfilling relationship.

Recognizing Love Languages in Others

Identifying the love languages of friends, family, and partners requires keen observation and thoughtful consideration. Use the following strategies to recognize and understand the love languages of those around you:

Observe Their Actions:

- Pay attention to how individuals express love through their actions.

- Notice gestures, behaviors, and activities that seem to bring them joy or fulfillment.

Listen to Their Expressions:

- Listen actively to their verbal expressions of love. Take note of the words they use to convey affection or appreciation.

- Observe whether they frequently use phrases related to love, encouragement, or support.

Note Their Preferred Expressions:

- Identify their preferred ways of expressing love. Do they often give compliments, perform acts of service, give thoughtful gifts, spend quality time, or engage in physical touch?

- Consider the consistency of these expressions across different situations.

Reflect on Their Reactions:

- Reflect on how individuals react to different expressions of love from others.

- Note their emotional responses, whether positive or negative, to various gestures and actions.

Consider Their Interests:

• Consider the activities or interests that bring them joy and fulfillment.

• Connect these preferences with the corresponding love languages. For example, someone who enjoys quality time may prioritize shared experiences.

Ask Direct Questions:

• Engage in open and honest conversations about love languages.

• Ask questions such as, "What makes you feel most loved?" or "How do you like to express love to others?"

Be Mindful of Cultural Differences:

• Recognize that cultural backgrounds can influence the ways people express and receive love.

• Consider how cultural factors may shape their preferences and interpretations of love languages.

Consider Their Childhood Experiences:

• Reflect on their childhood experiences and relationships, as these can influence their love language.

• Consider whether they may have developed certain preferences based on their upbringing.

Take Note of Relationship Dynamics:

• Observe how individuals interact within different relationships, such as with family, friends, and romantic partners.

• Note any patterns or consistencies in their expressions of love across different contexts.

Encourage Self-Reflection:

• Encourage individuals to reflect on their own love languages.

• Share resources, such as books or quizzes, that can assist them in understanding their preferred ways of giving and receiving love.

Navigating Relationship Challenges

Relationships are dynamic and may encounter challenges along the way. Here are strategies for navigating common relationship challenges:

Open Communication:

• Foster open and honest communication. Encourage a safe space for expressing feelings, concerns, and needs.

• Use "I" statements to avoid blame and promote understanding.

Active Listening:

• Practice active listening to truly understand your partner's perspective.

• Validate their feelings and show empathy to create a sense of mutual understanding.

Respect Differences:

• Acknowledge and respect the differences between you and your partner.
• Embrace diversity in thoughts, preferences, and communication styles.

Quality Time:

- Dedicate quality time to connect and nurture the relationship.

- Prioritize activities that strengthen your bond and create positive shared experiences.

Reaffirm Love Languages:

- Revisit and reaffirm each other's love languages. Understand how your partner expresses and receives love.

- Make intentional efforts to align with your partner's love language during challenging times.

Conflict Resolution:

- Develop healthy conflict resolution skills. Focus on finding solutions rather than escalating arguments.

- Take breaks if needed, but commit to returning to the conversation to reach a resolution.

Seek Professional Help:

- Consider seeking the guidance of a relationship counselor or therapist if challenges persist.

- Professional help can provide valuable insights and tools for navigating complex issues.

Express Appreciation:

- Regularly express appreciation for your partner. Acknowledge their efforts and contributions to the relationship.

- Cultivate a positive atmosphere by recognizing and celebrating each other.

Establish Boundaries:

• Establish clear and healthy boundaries in the relationship.

• Communicate your needs and expectations, and respect your partner's boundaries.

Cultivate Empathy:

• Cultivate empathy by putting yourself in your partner's shoes.

• Understand their perspective and emotions to strengthen the emotional connection.

Learn and Grow Together:

• View challenges as opportunities for growth. Learn and grow together through shared experiences.

• Approach difficulties as a team, reinforcing the idea that you are partners in navigating life's complexities.

Celebrate Achievements:

• Celebrate both individual and shared achievements.
• Recognize and support each other's personal growth and accomplishments.

Miscommunication and Love Languages

Miscommunication is a common challenge in relationships, often stemming from differences in communication styles and understanding of love languages. Here are strategies to address miscommunication related to love languages:

Increase Awareness:

- Foster awareness of your own love language and that of your partner.

- Recognize that miscommunication may arise when expressions of love are not aligned with the recipient's preferred love language.

Open Dialogue:

- Encourage open dialogue about love languages. Discuss your preferences and how you interpret expressions of love.

- Clarify any misunderstandings and share examples of what each love language means to you.

Educate Each Other:

- Take the time to educate each other on the nuances of your respective love languages.

- Share insights into the specific actions or words that resonate most deeply with you.

Observe Non-Verbal Cues:

- Pay attention to non-verbal cues and body language. Sometimes, miscommunication can be addressed by tuning into subtle expressions of emotion.

- Be receptive to the unspoken signals that convey your partner's feelings.

Ask for Clarification:

- If you sense miscommunication, ask for clarification rather than making assumptions.

- Seek to understand your partner's intentions and convey your own with clarity.

Practice Active Listening:

- Practice active listening to fully grasp your partner's perspective.

- Reflect back what you've heard to ensure mutual understanding and avoid misinterpretation.

Be Mindful of Timing:

- Be mindful of the timing of your expressions of love. Consider how the timing may impact your partner's ability to receive and appreciate them.

- Communicate openly about preferred timing for meaningful interactions.

Embrace Flexibility:

- Embrace flexibility in your approach to expressing love. Recognize that adapting your expressions to align with your partner's love language fosters better communication.

- Be willing to explore new ways of connecting.

Celebrate Differences:

- Celebrate the differences in your love languages as a source of richness in the relationship.

• Avoid viewing differences as obstacles, but rather as opportunities for learning and growth.

Reaffirm Love Languages:

• Regularly reaffirm your commitment to understanding and honoring each other's love languages.

• Make joint efforts to reinforce your expressions of love in ways that resonate with both partners.

Balancing Different Love Languages in a Relationship

Navigating a relationship with different love languages requires intentional efforts to ensure both partners feel loved and understood. Here are strategies for balancing different love languages:

Open Communication:

- Foster open and ongoing communication about love languages.

- Discuss your preferences, understand your partner's needs, and find common ground for expressing love.

Compromise and Flexibility:

- Embrace compromise and flexibility in expressing love. Find ways to incorporate elements of both partners' love languages into the relationship.

- Be open to experimenting with new ways of connecting.

Learn Each Other's Cues:

- Learn to recognize cues and signals that indicate your partner's need for love and affirmation.

- Be attuned to subtle expressions and adjust your approach accordingly.

Quality Time Integration:

- Integrate quality time into your routine, regardless of your primary love language.

- Find activities that both partners enjoy to create shared experiences.

Create a Balanced Routine:

- Establish a routine that balances expressions of love in alignment with each partner's love language.

- Consistently incorporate actions that resonate with both partners.

Celebrate Special Occasions:

- Make special occasions memorable by incorporating elements that cater to each other's love languages.

- Plan celebrations that reflect a thoughtful blend of both preferences.

Shared Love Language Activities:

- Identify activities that align with a shared love language and engage in them together.

- This could include acts of service, shared hobbies, or joint expressions of affection.

Regularly Reassess Preferences:

- Regularly reassess and discuss each other's love language preferences.

- Recognize that preferences may evolve over time, and staying attuned to these changes is crucial.

Seek Mutual Understanding:

- Foster mutual understanding and appreciation for the differences in love languages.

- Acknowledge that each partner's way of expressing love is valid and unique.

Implement Rituals:

• Establish rituals that incorporate elements of both love languages.

• This could include daily or weekly practices that cater to each partner's preferences.

Express Gratitude:

• Express gratitude for the efforts made by your partner to adapt and meet your love language.

• Acknowledge the intention behind their actions and appreciate the love they express.

Professional Guidance:

• Consider seeking the guidance of a relationship counselor or therapist if challenges persist.

• Professional assistance can provide tailored strategies for navigating differences in love languages.

Cultivating a Love Language-Focused Relationship

Building a love language-focused relationship involves intentional efforts to understand, appreciate, and cater to each other's preferred ways of giving and receiving love. Here are strategies for cultivating a love language-focused relationship:

Joint Exploration of Love Languages:

- Explore love languages together as a couple. Take quizzes and engage in conversations to understand each other's preferences.

- Use this shared understanding as a foundation for building a love language-focused relationship.

Regular Check-Ins:

- Schedule regular check-ins to discuss your emotional needs and any adjustments needed in expressing love.

- Ensure that both partners feel heard and supported in their love language preferences.

Create Love Language Rituals:

- Establish rituals that specifically cater to each other's love languages.

- These rituals could include weekly acts of service, daily affirmations, or planned quality time.

Celebrate Love Language Milestones:

- Celebrate relationship milestones by incorporating expressions of love in alignment with each other's love languages.

• Recognize the importance of these milestones in strengthening the bond between partners.

Shared Love Language Goals:

• Set joint goals for integrating love languages into your daily life.

• Work collaboratively to create an environment that nurtures and supports each partner's preferred expressions of love.

Surprise Gestures:

• Incorporate surprise gestures aligned with your partner's love language.

• These surprises can be thoughtful acts of service, special gifts, or planned moments of quality time.

Express Appreciation for Efforts:

• Express gratitude for your partner's efforts to align with your love language.

• Acknowledge the intention and care behind their actions, reinforcing a positive cycle of love expression.

Adapt to Life Changes:

• Recognize that life circumstances and priorities may change. Be adaptable in adjusting your expressions of love to accommodate these changes.

• Communicate openly about how love languages may evolve over time.

Quality Time Escapes:

- Plan occasional escapes or activities that cater to the shared love language of quality time.

- Create opportunities to deepen your emotional connection through focused and undistracted time together.

Explore New Love Language Expressions:

- Be open to exploring new ways of expressing love that may align with your partner's evolving preferences.

- Encourage a sense of curiosity and creativity in discovering new expressions of love.

Celebrate Individuality:

- Celebrate and honor each other's individuality in terms of love languages.

- Avoid comparison or judgment, recognizing that diverse expressions of love contribute to the uniqueness of the relationship.

Prioritize Emotional Well-Being:

- Prioritize each other's emotional well-being by consistently attending to love language needs.

- Cultivate an environment where both partners feel emotionally supported and fulfilled.

Love Languages in Various Relationships

Love languages play a significant role in various types of relationships, influencing how individuals express and receive love. Here's how love languages manifest in different relationship contexts:

Romantic Partnerships:

• In romantic relationships, understanding and aligning with each other's love languages are crucial.

• Partners may express love through acts of service, words of affirmation, quality time, physical touch, or the exchange of thoughtful gifts.

Friendships:

• Love languages also apply to friendships, influencing the ways friends connect and show appreciation.

• Friends may express love through quality time spent together, words of affirmation, or thoughtful acts that cater to each other's preferences.

Family Dynamics:

• Within families, individuals often have different love languages.

• Parents may express love to children through acts of service, while children may have their own unique ways of showing love, such as spending quality time.

Siblings:

• Siblings may have distinct love languages, leading to varied expressions of affection.

• Some siblings may prioritize quality time, while others may show love through acts of service or sharing thoughtful gifts.

Workplace Relationships:

• Love languages can influence professional relationships, impacting how colleagues and team members express appreciation.

• Recognition of achievements, words of affirmation, or collaborative efforts (acts of service) can contribute to positive workplace dynamics.

Parent-Child Relationships:

• Love languages guide the parent-child dynamic, influencing how parents express affection and how children interpret love.

• Parents may express love through providing quality time, while children may have their preferred ways of receiving love, such as words of affirmation.

Extended Family:

• Extended family relationships may involve diverse love languages among relatives.

• Celebrations and gatherings provide opportunities for expressing love through shared experiences, thoughtful gifts, and affirming words.

Close Friendships:

• Love languages influence the depth of connection in close friendships.

• Friends may navigate conflict and celebrate achievements by using each other's love languages for support and affirmation.

Mentor-mentee Relationships:

• In mentor-mentee relationships, understanding love languages contributes to effective communication and support.

• Mentors may guide and affirm their mentees, while mentees may express appreciation through acts of service or thoughtful gestures.

Community and Social Groups:

• Love languages are present in community and social groups, impacting the dynamics and sense of belonging.

• Group members may express love through collective quality time, shared activities, or supportive words.

Love Languages in Family Dynamics

Love languages play a crucial role in shaping the dynamics within a family. Each family member may have unique preferences for expressing and receiving love. Here's how love languages manifest in family relationships:

Parent-Child Relationships:

- Parents may express love through acts of service, such as preparing meals or helping with homework.

- Children may have different love language preferences, with some valuing quality time or words of affirmation from their parents.

Sibling Relationships:

- Siblings may have distinct love languages that influence their interactions.

- Some siblings may express love through acts of service, like helping with chores, while others may prioritize quality time spent together.

Quality Time in Families:

- Quality time is a common love language within families, involving shared activities and meaningful experiences.

- Family outings, game nights, or simply spending time together contribute to a sense of connection and love.

Words of Affirmation:

- Words of affirmation are significant in family dynamics, with expressions of love and encouragement contributing to positive relationships.

- Compliments, expressions of pride, and verbal affirmations strengthen the emotional bonds within the family.

Acts of Service:

- Acts of service within families involve actions that show thoughtfulness and consideration.

- Parents may perform acts of service for their children, such as assisting with school projects or helping with daily tasks.

Receiving Gifts:

- The love language of receiving gifts may involve thoughtful gestures within the family.

- Celebrating special occasions with meaningful gifts or expressing love through small surprises contributes to a positive family environment.

Physical Touch:

- Physical touch is a love language that manifests through affectionate gestures within families.

- Hugs, kisses, and physical closeness contribute to a sense of security and love among family members.

Understanding Children's Love Languages:

- Parents benefit from understanding their children's love languages to tailor expressions of love accordingly.

- Observing how children respond to different forms of affection helps parents nurture a strong emotional connection.

Adapting to Changes:

• Family dynamics may change over time due to life events or transitions.

• Adapting expressions of love to align with changing circumstances helps maintain a sense of connection within the family.

Conflict Resolution through Love Languages:

• Understanding each family member's love language aids in conflict resolution.

• Addressing conflicts with consideration for individual preferences helps navigate challenges more effectively.

Cultural Influences on Love Languages:

• Cultural backgrounds can influence the ways family members express and receive love.

• Being mindful of cultural differences enhances understanding and respect within the family.

Love Languages in Friendships

Love languages are not exclusive to romantic relationships; they also play a significant role in shaping the dynamics of friendships. Here's how love languages manifest in different aspects of friendships:

Words of Affirmation:

- Friends may express love through affirming words, providing encouragement, and offering positive feedback.

- Compliments, expressions of support, and verbal encouragement strengthen the bond between friends.

Quality Time:

- Quality time is a common love language in friendships, involving shared experiences and meaningful interactions.

- Friends may prioritize spending time together, and engaging in activities they both enjoy.

Acts of Service:

- Acts of service in friendships involve thoughtful gestures and actions that demonstrate care.

- Helping a friend with tasks, offering assistance during challenging times, or providing practical support are expressions of love.

Receiving Gifts:

- The love language of receiving gifts may involve thoughtful exchanges that convey appreciation and consideration.

- Friends may express love through giving meaningful gifts on special occasions or as spontaneous gestures.

Physical Touch:

• Physical touch plays a role in some friendships, involving expressions of affection such as hugs or pats on the back.

• Friends who share this love language may feel a stronger connection through physical closeness.

Understanding Personal Boundaries:

• Recognizing and respecting personal boundaries is crucial in friendships.

• Friends should be aware of each other's comfort levels regarding expressions of love, especially in terms of physical touch.

Adapting to Different Preferences:

• Friends may have different love language preferences.

• Adapting expressions of love to align with the unique preferences of each friend contributes to stronger and more meaningful friendships.

Celebrating Achievements:

• Friends express love by celebrating each other's achievements and milestones.

• Recognizing and commemorating successes fosters a supportive and affirming friendship.

Open Communication:

• Effective communication is essential in friendships, especially regarding love languages.

• Friends benefit from openly discussing their preferences, ensuring mutual understanding and connection.

Navigating Conflicts:

• Understanding each other's love languages aids in navigating conflicts.

• Friends can approach conflicts with consideration for how their expressions of love may impact the resolution process.

Cultural Influences:

• Cultural backgrounds may influence the ways friends express and interpret love.

• Being mindful of cultural differences enhances understanding and fosters a more inclusive and respectful friendship.

Long-Distance Friendships:

• In long-distance friendships, love languages can be expressed through virtual means, such as video calls, messages, and sending surprise gifts.

• Adapting expressions of love to the challenges of distance maintains a strong connection.

Applying Love Languages in Professional Relationships

While the concept of love languages is often associated with personal relationships, elements of it can be applied to enhance professional relationships and workplace dynamics. Here's how love languages can be relevant in a professional context:

Words of Affirmation:

- Expressing appreciation and providing positive feedback to colleagues can create a supportive work environment.

- Recognize and acknowledge the efforts and achievements of team members through verbal affirmations.

Quality Time:

- Foster team building and collaboration by investing quality time in joint projects and shared activities.

- Prioritize regular team meetings and one-on-one discussions to strengthen interpersonal connections.

Acts of Service:

- Demonstrating acts of service can contribute to a positive work atmosphere.

- Offering assistance, sharing workload, or providing support during challenging tasks can enhance team cohesion.

Receiving Gifts:

- Although physical gifts may not be as common in professional settings, symbolic gestures can convey appreciation.

• Recognize accomplishments with tokens of recognition or celebrate milestones to show gratitude.

Physical Touch:

• In a professional context, physical touch is replaced by non-physical forms of connection.

• Express empathy and camaraderie through gestures like handshakes, fist bumps, or other appropriate non-verbal cues.

Understanding Individual Preferences:

• Recognize that team members may have diverse love language preferences.

• Encourage open communication about preferred modes of recognition and support within the professional setting.

Celebrating Achievements:

• Celebrate team achievements and individual accomplishments within the workplace.

• Recognition ceremonies, awards, or public acknowledgment contribute to a positive and affirming work culture.

Open Communication:

• Encourage open communication among team members to understand each other's expectations and preferences.

• Regularly seek feedback and ensure that team members feel heard and valued.

Quality Interactions:

- Prioritize quality interactions during meetings and collaborative sessions.

- Create an environment where team members feel comfortable expressing ideas, sharing concerns, and engaging in constructive discussions.

Cultural Sensitivity:

- Be mindful of cultural differences within the professional setting.

- Recognize and respect diverse ways in which individuals may prefer to give and receive recognition.

Mentorship and Guidance:

- In mentor-mentee relationships, understanding each other's communication preferences is crucial.

- Mentors can provide guidance and support aligned with the mentee's love language for effective professional development.

Flexibility and Adaptability:

- Recognize that individuals may have changing preferences over time.

- Be flexible and adaptable in adjusting your expressions of appreciation to align with evolving needs.

Case Studies

Case Study 1: Workplace Harmony

Background:

Susan and James work together in a fast-paced marketing agency. They often collaborate on projects, but recently, there's been tension in their communication.

Scenario:

Susan prefers words of affirmation, and James values acts of service. Susan feels unappreciated because James rarely compliments her work. On the other hand, James feels overwhelmed with tasks and wishes Susan would offer practical help instead of just words.

Application of Love Languages:

• Understanding Preferences: Susan and James attend a team-building workshop that includes a session on love languages. They realize the difference in their preferences – Susan values affirming words, and James appreciates practical support.

• Adapting Communication: Susan begins to express appreciation for James's efforts verbally, while James actively looks for opportunities to assist Susan in tasks, understanding that this is how they both feel valued.

• Team Integration: The team, aware of each other's love languages, starts incorporating diverse expressions of appreciation. This leads to improved collaboration, reduced tension, and a more positive work atmosphere.

Case Study 2: Family Connection

Background:

The Thompson family consists of parents, Mark and Emily, and their two teenage children, Olivia and Jake. Lately, the family has been feeling disconnected due to busy schedules and conflicting priorities.

Scenario:

Mark's love language is quality time, Emily values acts of service, Olivia appreciates words of affirmation, and Jake leans towards physical touch. The family struggles to find common ground and often feels misunderstood.

Application of Love Languages:

• Family Meeting: The Thompsons decide to have a family meeting to discuss their love languages. Each member shares their preferences and how they feel loved.

• Customized Expressions: Mark plans weekly family outings for quality time, Emily takes on tasks to help alleviate everyone's workload, Olivia and Jake express their needs more clearly, and the family starts incorporating hugs and physical touch in daily interactions.

• Regular Check-Ins: The family establishes a routine of regular check-ins to ensure they are meeting each other's emotional needs. They celebrate achievements and express gratitude using the appropriate love languages.

Example 1: Couple's Communication

Background:

Sarah and John have been married for several years. Sarah's primary love language is acts of service, while John's is words of affirmation.

Example:

One day, John notices that Sarah has had a particularly stressful week at work. Instead of just expressing verbal support, John takes the initiative to handle some household chores that Sarah usually does. He prepares dinner, does the dishes, and takes care of a few tasks that were on Sarah's to-do list.

Sarah, feeling overwhelmed, comes home to find a clean house and a thoughtfully prepared meal. Instead of just saying, "Thank you," John also verbally affirms Sarah, telling her how much he appreciates her hard work and how proud he is of her accomplishments.

In this example, John combines Sarah's love language of acts of service with his own love language of words of affirmation. This thoughtful combination enhances their communication and strengthens their emotional connection.

Example 2: Parent-Child Bonding

Background:

The Rodriguez family consists of parents, Maria and Carlos, and their teenage daughter, Sofia. Sofia's primary love language is quality time, while her parents both lean towards acts of service.

Example:

One weekend, Sofia expresses a desire to spend more quality time with her parents. Instead of just planning activities, Maria and Carlos decide to integrate their acts of service and love language into the quality time experience.

They organize a family picnic in the park, where Maria and Carlos prepare Sofia's favorite dishes. During the picnic, they engage in quality conversations, making an effort to understand Sofia's thoughts and feelings. After the picnic, Carlos surprises Sofia by helping her with a project she's been working on for school.

In this example, Maria and Carlos bridge the gap between Sofia's love language and their own by combining acts of service with quality time. This holistic approach allows them to connect on multiple levels, creating a meaningful and fulfilling family experience.

Overcoming Challenges through Love Language Awareness

Challenges in relationships are inevitable, but love language awareness can be a powerful tool for overcoming them. Here's how individuals and couples can navigate difficulties by understanding and applying their love languages:
Communication Breakdowns:

- Challenge: Miscommunication can lead to misunderstandings and conflicts.

- Love Language Solution: Couples can proactively discuss their love languages to enhance communication. For example, if one partner values quality time, scheduling regular check-ins can provide a dedicated space for open communication.

Feeling Unappreciated:

- Challenge: Partners may feel unappreciated if their preferred love language is not acknowledged.

- Love Language Solution: Expressing gratitude in a way that aligns with the partner's love language can address this challenge. If one partner values acts of service, recognizing their efforts with verbal affirmations enhances feelings of appreciation.

Differing Priorities:

- Challenge: Individuals may prioritize different aspects of the relationship, leading to feelings of neglect.

- Love Language Solution: Understanding each other's love languages helps couples navigate differing priorities. They can then intentionally incorporate expressions of love that resonate with both partners, ensuring a balance in meeting each other's emotional needs.

Stress and Busyness:

- Challenge: Stress and busy schedules can strain relationships, leading to emotional distance.

- Love Language Solution: Couples can address this challenge by recognizing stress triggers and actively incorporating stress-relieving activities aligned with their love languages. For instance, a partner who values physical touch may find comfort in hugs during stressful times.

Rekindling Romance:

- Challenge: Over time, couples may feel a decline in the romantic aspect of their relationship.

- Love Language Solution: Rekindling romance involves understanding each other's romantic preferences. Planning surprise gestures, gifts, or intimate quality time can reignite the passion and strengthen the emotional connection.

Parent-Child Relationship Struggles:

- Challenge: Parenting challenges can strain the parent-child relationship.

- Love Language Solution: Parents can navigate these challenges by understanding their children's love languages. Tailoring expressions of love, such as providing words of affirmation or engaging in quality time activities, helps build a supportive parent-child bond.

Maintaining Friendships:

- Challenge: Busy schedules may lead to neglect in maintaining friendships.

• Love Language Solution: Friends can overcome this challenge by staying connected through methods that align with their love languages. For example, scheduling regular video calls for quality time or sending thoughtful messages for words of affirmation.

Adjusting to Life Changes:

• Challenge: Major life changes, such as relocation or career shifts, can impact relationships.

• Love Language Solution: Couples facing life changes can adapt by openly discussing their evolving needs and adjusting expressions of love accordingly. This helps maintain a sense of connection and support during transitions.

Cultivating a Love Language-Rich Environment

Creating an environment that embraces and supports love languages involves intentional efforts to understand, appreciate, and express love in ways that resonate with individuals. Here's a guide on cultivating a love language-rich environment:

Self-Reflection:

• Begin by individually reflecting on your own love language preferences. Identify the primary ways you prefer to give and receive love.

Open Communication:

• Foster open communication within relationships. Encourage discussions about love languages to understand each other's preferences and expectations.

Love Language Quizzes:

• Take love language quizzes together as a group, whether it's with family, friends, or colleagues. This shared activity promotes awareness and understanding of each other's love languages.

Individual and Group Acknowledgment:

• Acknowledge and appreciate each individual's unique love language within the group. Recognize that diverse expressions of love contribute to a rich and supportive environment.

Customized Expressions:

• Tailor expressions of love to align with each person's love language. This could involve offering words of affirmation, acts of service, quality time, physical touch, or thoughtful gifts based on individual preferences.

Celebrating Milestones:

• Celebrate personal and collective milestones within the group. Acknowledge achievements using expressions of love that resonate with the individuals involved.

Quality Time Rituals:

• Establish rituals that involve quality time spent together. This could include regular group activities, shared meals, or dedicated moments for meaningful conversations.

Acts of Service Integration:

• Integrate acts of service into the group dynamic. Support each other through helpful actions that cater to individual needs and preferences.

Group Dynamics Check-Ins:

• Conduct periodic check-ins on group dynamics. Encourage members to share their feelings and experiences, providing an opportunity to adjust expressions of love as needed.

Flexibility and Adaptability:

• Remain flexible and adaptable in accommodating changing circumstances. Life events, personal growth, and evolving preferences may impact love languages, requiring adjustments for continued connection.

Expressing Gratitude:

• Cultivate a culture of gratitude within the group. Encourage the expression of appreciation for each other's contributions and expressions of love.

Educational Sessions:

• Host educational sessions or workshops on love languages. This can deepen understanding, promote empathy, and reinforce the importance of creating a love language-rich environment.

Personal Development Support:

• Support each other's personal development by acknowledging and respecting changes in love language preferences over time. Create an atmosphere that embraces growth and evolving expressions of love.

Inclusive Approach:

• Ensure inclusivity by recognizing and respecting diverse cultural backgrounds and individual differences. A love language-rich environment is one that accommodates various expressions and interpretations of love.

Creating Rituals and Traditions that Reflect Love Languages

Establishing rituals and traditions that align with love languages can deepen emotional connections and create meaningful experiences within relationships. Here are ideas for creating love language-centered rituals and traditions:

Quality Time Rituals:

- Weekly Movie Night: Dedicate a specific night each week for a movie night. Choose films that cater to everyone's preferences, ensuring quality time together.

- Nature Walks or Hikes: Incorporate regular nature walks or hikes into your routine. This provides an opportunity for quality time in a serene environment.

Words of Affirmation Traditions:

- Gratitude Circle: Before family meals or gatherings, establish a tradition where each member shares something they're grateful for, offering words of affirmation to one another.

- Annual Appreciation Letters: On special occasions, such as birthdays or anniversaries, exchange handwritten letters expressing affirmations and appreciation.

Acts of Service Rituals:

- Family Chore Day: Designate a day each month for a family chore day where everyone contributes to acts of service, helping each other with tasks around the house.

- Meal Prep Together: Collaborate on preparing meals together. This not only involves acts of service but also provides quality time spent as a team.

Receiving Gifts Traditions:

• Surprise Gift Days: Establish surprise gift days where family members exchange small, thoughtful gifts. These gestures can be tokens of appreciation.

• Memory Boxes: Create memory boxes for each family member. Regularly add small, symbolic gifts that hold sentimental value to celebrate shared experiences.

Physical Touch Rituals:

• Family Hug Circle: Initiate a family hug circle before bedtime or in the morning. This physical touch ritual fosters a sense of warmth and connection.

• High-Five Ritual: Incorporate a daily or weekly high-five ritual. This simple physical touch can serve as a quick, positive affirmation.

Combined Love Languages Traditions:

• Annual Retreat or Getaway: Plan an annual family retreat or getaway that incorporates elements catering to each love language. This could include quality time, acts of service, words of affirmation, and thoughtful gifts.

• Celebration Jar: Maintain a celebration jar where family members can drop notes of achievements or positive experiences. Periodically, gather to read and celebrate these moments together.

Celebrating Individuality:

• Personalized Birthday Celebrations: Tailor birthday celebrations to each individual's love language. For example, a surprise party for one, a heartfelt letter for another, or a day of quality time for someone else.

- Customized Holiday Traditions: Modify holiday traditions to reflect the love languages of each family member. This could involve adjusting gift-giving practices, incorporating specific activities, or emphasizing quality time.

Reflective Self-Care:

- Individual Self-Care Days: Designate days where each family member gets to choose activities that align with their love language for self-care. This promotes self-awareness and encourages the practice of self-love.

Celebrating Special Moments in Alignment with Love Languages

Tailoring celebrations to align with love languages enhances the meaningfulness of special moments. Here are ways to celebrate important occasions while considering various love languages:

Quality Time Celebration:

- Plan a day trip or weekend getaway to spend quality time together.

- Organize a family game night or movie marathon, focusing on shared experiences.

Words of Affirmation Celebration:

- Write a heartfelt letter expressing appreciation and love.

- Create a customized playlist with songs that hold sentimental value, accompanied by a note explaining each selection.

Acts of Service Celebration:

- Surprise with a day where you take care of tasks they usually handle.

- Cook a special meal or organize a celebratory dinner to alleviate their responsibilities.

Receiving Gifts Celebration:

- Select a thoughtful and meaningful gift that reflects their interests.

- Create a personalized gift, such as a scrapbook or photo album, capturing cherished memories.

Physical Touch Celebration:

- Plan a day of physical activities or adventures, like hiking or dancing.

- Gift a cozy blanket or massage session for a relaxing and physical touch-oriented celebration.

Combination Celebration:

- Design a celebration that incorporates elements of multiple love languages.

- For example, a surprise picnic (acts of service) in a scenic location with shared quality time, accompanied by a heartfelt letter (words of affirmation).

Family Celebration:

- Organize a family gathering or reunion, emphasizing quality time and connections.

- Collaborate on a group project or activity that involves acts of service, such as gardening or home improvement.

Birthday Celebration:

- Customize birthday celebrations based on individual love languages.

- Host a surprise party for those who enjoy socializing, plan a quiet day for introverts, or organize a themed event for those who appreciate creative expressions.

Anniversary Celebration:

- Reflect on shared memories and express words of affirmation in a heartfelt letter or speech.

• Plan an intimate dinner or getaway, focusing on quality time and celebrating the journey together.

Graduation Celebration:

• Acknowledge achievements through affirming words in a congratulatory card or speech.

• Gift a symbol of accomplishment, such as a personalized item or a book related to their interests.

Promotion or Career Milestone Celebration:

• Organize a surprise gathering with colleagues to celebrate achievements socially.

• Provide support through acts of service, such as helping with workload during a busy time.

Holiday Celebration:

• Tailor holiday traditions to incorporate love languages.

• Plan activities that resonate with each family member's preferences, ensuring an inclusive and joyful celebration.

Sustaining a Love Language-Centric Lifestyle

Maintaining a love language-centric lifestyle involves ongoing commitment and intentional efforts to prioritize and express love in ways that resonate with individuals. Here are strategies to sustain a love language-centric lifestyle:

Regular Check-Ins:

- Conduct regular check-ins with yourself and your loved ones to reassess love language preferences.

- Communicate openly about any changes or evolving needs, ensuring that expressions of love remain aligned with current preferences.

Celebrate Small Moments:

- Incorporate love language expressions into daily routines and small moments.

- Celebrate achievements, express gratitude, or engage in acts of service in the ordinary moments of life to maintain a consistent love-centric lifestyle.

Scheduled Quality Time:

- Schedule dedicated quality time regularly. This can be a weekly family dinner, a monthly outing, or a quarterly weekend getaway.

- Prioritize these scheduled moments to reinforce the importance of quality time in your relationships.

Surprise Gestures:

- Integrate surprise gestures aligned with love languages.

• Periodically surprise your loved ones with thoughtful gifts, acts of service, or words of affirmation to keep the love language-centric lifestyle dynamic and exciting.

Incorporate Love Languages into Daily Rituals:

• Weave love language expressions into daily rituals and routines.

• For example, start the day with words of affirmation, share acts of service during meal preparations, and end the day with quality time activities.

Flexibility and Adaptability:

• Remain flexible and adaptable to changes in preferences or life circumstances.

• Adjust expressions of love accordingly, ensuring that they remain relevant and supportive of each individual's emotional needs.

Mindful Communication:

• Practice mindful communication to deepen understanding.

• Regularly check in with your loved ones about their emotional well-being, encouraging open dialogue about how love languages are being expressed and received.

Create Love Language Rituals:

• Establish specific rituals or traditions that embody love language expressions.

• This could include a monthly appreciation circle, a surprise gesture day, or a family project that incorporates acts of service.

Celebrate Love Language Anniversaries:

- Acknowledge and celebrate the anniversary of discovering and understanding each other's love languages.

- Use this time to reflect on the positive impact of incorporating love languages into your lifestyle.

Continuous Learning:

- Stay informed and engaged with resources related to love languages.

- Read books, attend workshops, or participate in discussions to deepen your understanding and refine your ability to express love in meaningful ways.

Encourage Individual Self-Care:

- Support each other in practicing self-love and self-care aligned with love languages.

- Encourage individual well-being to sustain a healthy and love language-centric lifestyle.

Lead by Example:

- Demonstrate love language expressions through your own actions.

- By consistently embodying the love languages, you inspire others to reciprocate and contribute to a love-centric lifestyle.

Future Trends in Love Languages Research

Predicting future trends in love languages research involves considering evolving societal dynamics, technological advancements, and shifts in interpersonal relationships. Here are potential areas of focus for future research on love languages:

Digital Expression of Love:

- Explore how digital communication platforms and technology influence the expression and interpretation of love languages.

- Investigate the impact of emojis, virtual gestures, and online interactions on the perception of love languages.

Cultural Variations:

- Conduct cross-cultural studies to understand how love languages manifest in different cultural contexts.

- Explore the influence of cultural norms and values on the development and expression of love languages.

Neuroscience and Love Languages:

- Investigate the neural mechanisms associated with different love languages.

- Use neuroimaging techniques to explore brain activity during experiences related to words of affirmation, acts of service, quality time, receiving gifts, and physical touch.

Generational Shifts:

- Examine how love languages evolve across different generations.

- Explore whether societal changes, technological advancements, or cultural shifts impact the development and prioritization of love languages in younger generations.

Love Languages in Virtual Relationships:

- Investigate how love languages play a role in virtual relationships, including online friendships, long-distance relationships, and digital connections.

- Explore the challenges and opportunities for expressing love languages in virtual spaces.

Personalized Love Language Assessments:

- Develop and refine personalized love language assessments that consider individual nuances and preferences.

- Explore the integration of technology, such as artificial intelligence, in creating more accurate and tailored assessments.

Love Languages in Professional Settings:

- Explore the application of love languages in workplace dynamics and professional relationships.

- Investigate how understanding and incorporating love languages can contribute to employee satisfaction, team cohesion, and organizational culture.

Impact of External Factors:

- Examine how external factors, such as economic conditions, political climates, or global events, influence the prioritization and expression of love languages.

- Explore the resilience of love languages in the face of external stressors.

Long-Term Effects of Love Language Alignment:

- Conduct longitudinal studies to explore the long-term effects of aligning expressions of love with individuals' love languages.

• Investigate the impact on relationship satisfaction, mental health, and overall well-being over extended periods.

Intergenerational Transmission of Love Languages:

• Explore how love languages are transmitted across generations within families.

• Investigate the role of parental modeling and the impact of childhood experiences on the development of individuals' love languages.

Mindfulness and Love Languages:

• Investigate the relationship between mindfulness practices and the conscious expression of love languages.

• Explore how mindfulness techniques can enhance individuals' awareness and responsiveness to love language preferences.

Love Languages and Mental Health:

• Explore the connection between love languages and mental health outcomes.

• Investigate how expressing and receiving love in alignment with one's love language may contribute to emotional well-being and resilience.

Digital Communication and Love Languages:

• Explore how the rise of digital communication platforms, social media, and virtual interactions impact the expression and understanding of love languages.

Impact of the COVID-19 Pandemic:

• Investigate how the pandemic has influenced the prioritization and expression of love languages, especially considering changes in social dynamics, increased reliance on technology, and altered work-life balances.

Neuroscientific Insights:

• Explore neuroscientific studies that delve into the neural correlates of love languages, providing a deeper understanding of the brain mechanisms associated with different expressions of love.

Applications in Therapy and Counseling:

• Examine how knowledge of love languages is integrated into therapeutic practices and counseling settings. Explore its effectiveness in improving communication and relationship satisfaction.

Love Languages in Diverse Relationships:

• Investigate how love languages manifest in diverse relationship structures, including non-traditional family dynamics, polyamorous relationships, and various forms of partnerships.

Technological Innovations in Love Language Assessments:

• Explore advancements in technology and data analytics to develop more sophisticated and personalized assessments of love languages, offering individuals tailored insights into their preferences.

Intergenerational Transmission of Love Languages:

• Investigate how love languages are passed down from one generation to the next, exploring the role of parental modeling and the impact of childhood experiences on the development of love languages.

Mindfulness and Love Languages:

- Explore studies that examine the relationship between mindfulness practices and the conscious expression of love languages, investigating how mindfulness may enhance individuals' awareness and responsiveness.

Cross-Cultural Studies:

- Conduct cross-cultural studies to understand variations in the manifestation and importance of love languages across different cultural contexts.

Longitudinal Studies on Relationship Outcomes:

- Undertake longitudinal studies to explore the long-term impact of aligning expressions of love with individuals' love languages on relationship satisfaction, mental health, and overall well-being.

Impact of Gender and Identity:

- Investigate how gender identity and expression may intersect with love languages, considering the nuanced ways in which individuals of diverse gender identities experience and express love.

Love Languages in Aging Populations:

- Explore the role of love languages in the relationships of aging populations, considering how expressions of love may evolve over the lifespan.

Shift Toward Individuality:

- Traditional Roles: There's a departure from traditional gender roles and expectations in relationships. Individuals are seeking partnerships based on shared values, interests, and personal fulfillment rather than adhering to predefined roles.

Focus on Equality and Partnership:

- Gender Equality: There's a growing emphasis on equality and partnership in relationships. Couples are more likely to share responsibilities, and decision-making, and contribute to each other's personal and professional growth.

Diversity and Inclusivity:

- Recognition of Diverse Relationships: Evolving perspectives acknowledge and celebrate diverse relationship structures, including non-heteronormative relationships, polyamory, and various forms of partnerships.

Impact of Technology:

- Digital Connections: Technology has changed the landscape of dating and relationships. Online dating, social media, and communication platforms play a significant role in how individuals meet, connect, and maintain relationships.

Delayed Marriage and Family Planning:

- Changing Life Priorities: Many individuals are prioritizing personal and career development before marriage. There's a trend toward later marriages and delayed family planning as people pursue educational and professional goals.

Emphasis on Communication:

- Open Communication: Communication is viewed as a cornerstone of healthy relationships. Couples are encouraged to communicate openly about needs, expectations, and emotions to foster understanding and intimacy.

Individual Well-Being:

- Self-Love and Self-Care: There's an increased emphasis on individual well-being. Healthy relationships are seen as those that support personal growth, self-love, and self-care rather than relying solely on the relationship for fulfillment.

Mindfulness in Relationships:

• Present Moment Awareness: Mindfulness practices are integrated into relationship perspectives, encouraging individuals to be present in their interactions, appreciate the current moment, and cultivate gratitude for their partners.

Rethinking Monogamy:

• Exploration of Non-Traditional Structures: Some individuals are challenging traditional notions of monogamy. Open relationships, ethical non-monogamy, and consensual non-monogamy are topics of discussion and exploration.

Impact of Social Movements:

• Intersectionality in Relationships: Social justice movements have influenced perspectives on intersectionality within relationships. There's a recognition of the intersection of identities and how they shape individuals' experiences in relationships.

Personalized Relationship Models:

• Tailoring Relationship Structures: There's a move toward personalized relationship models that cater to the unique needs and preferences of individuals and couples, allowing for greater flexibility in defining what works for them.

Embracing Imperfections:

• Realistic Expectations: Evolving perspectives acknowledge that relationships are not perfect. There's a shift toward embracing imperfections, accepting challenges, and working collaboratively to navigate difficulties.

Cultural Sensitivity:

- Respecting Cultural Differences: Perspectives on love and relationships take into account cultural diversity. There's an awareness of how cultural backgrounds influence relationship dynamics and practices.

The emphasis on individuality, equality, and partnership reflects a departure from rigid gender roles, allowing for relationships to be built on shared values and mutual fulfillment. Diversity and inclusivity are celebrated, recognizing a wide spectrum of relationship structures beyond the traditional norm.

Technology has become a significant force in shaping how individuals connect, meet, and maintain relationships. Digital platforms play a crucial role in the modern dating landscape, influencing the ways people initiate and sustain romantic connections.

Delayed marriage and family planning are part of a broader trend where individuals prioritize personal and professional development before settling into long-term commitments. Open communication is regarded as fundamental, fostering understanding and intimacy within relationships.

The focus on individual well-being has given rise to a culture of self-love and self-care. Mindfulness practices are integrated into relationship perspectives, encouraging present-moment awareness and gratitude for the experiences shared with partners.

Challenging traditional notions of monogamy, some individuals explore non-traditional relationship structures, such as open relationships or ethical non-monogamy. Social movements have influenced discussions on intersectionality within relationships, acknowledging the diverse identities that shape individuals' experiences.

Personalized relationship models allow couples to tailor their partnerships to meet their unique needs and preferences, fostering greater flexibility in defining the parameters of their relationships. There's a growing acceptance of imperfections, with a realistic understanding that relationships require effort, communication, and the ability to navigate challenges together.

Cultural sensitivity plays a crucial role in recognizing and respecting the influence of diverse cultural backgrounds on relationship dynamics. The evolving perspectives on love and relationships collectively contribute to a more nuanced and inclusive understanding, embracing the diversity of human experiences in the realm of love.

Key Takeaways:

Individuality and Equality:

- Evolving perspectives on love and relationships emphasize individuality, departing from traditional gender roles.

- There is a focus on equality and partnership, with shared responsibilities and contributions to personal growth.

Diversity and Inclusivity:

- Celebrating diverse relationship structures, including non-traditional forms such as polyamory and varied partnerships.

- Recognition of the impact of cultural diversity on relationship dynamics.

Technology's Influence:

- Technology, including online dating and social media, plays a significant role in how individuals connect and maintain relationships.

Delayed Marriage and Personal Priorities:

- A trend towards delayed marriage and family planning as individuals prioritize personal and career development.

Communication and Mindfulness:

- Open communication is fundamental, with a focus on expressing needs and emotions openly.

- Integration of mindfulness practices into relationships, emphasizing present-moment awareness and gratitude.

Challenges to Traditional Monogamy:

- Exploration of non-traditional relationship structures, challenging conventional notions of monogamy.

- Recognition of imperfections in relationships and a realistic understanding of challenges.

Personalized Relationship Models:

- Adoption of personalized relationship models that cater to unique needs and preferences.

- Flexibility in defining relationship parameters based on individual and collective desires.

Cultural Sensitivity:

- Respect for cultural differences and acknowledgment of how cultural backgrounds influence relationship dynamics.

Embracing Imperfections:

- Shift towards accepting imperfections in relationships and understanding that challenges are a natural part of the journey.

Focus on Individual Well-Being:

- Emphasis on self-love and self-care as integral components of maintaining healthy relationships.

Intersectionality in Relationships:

• Recognition of the intersectionality of identities within relationships, influenced by social justice movements.

Exploring and understanding love languages is a journey that can bring depth and richness to your relationships. Here's some encouragement to embark on this exploration:

Enhanced Connection:

• Discovering and understanding your own love language, as well as those of your loved ones, can significantly enhance your connection. It provides insight into how you give and receive love, fostering a deeper emotional bond.

Effective Communication:

• Love languages offer a framework for effective communication. By expressing love in ways that resonate with your partner's language, you create a more meaningful and fulfilling connection.

Personal Growth:

• Exploring love languages can be a journey of self-discovery. Understanding your preferences and needs in a relationship contributes to personal growth and self-awareness.

Resilience in Relationships:

• Knowledge of love languages equips you with tools to navigate challenges and conflicts in relationships. It promotes resilience by fostering understanding and empathy.

Celebrating Differences:

• Love languages celebrate the uniqueness of individuals. Embracing diverse expressions of love allows for a more inclusive and accepting approach to relationships.

Mindful Intimacy:

• Mindfully incorporating love languages into your relationship promotes intimate connections. It encourages thoughtful gestures and genuine expressions of affection.

Tailoring Expressions:

• Love language exploration enables you to tailor your expressions of love. Whether through words of affirmation, acts of service, quality time, receiving gifts, or physical touch, you can customize your approach to match your partner's preferences.

Building a Love Language Culture:

• Creating a love language-centric environment fosters a culture of appreciation and understanding. It contributes to a positive atmosphere where love is expressed in ways that resonate with each individual.

Adaptable and Evolving:

• Love languages are adaptable and can evolve. Embrace the fluidity of preferences and be open to discovering new aspects of yourself and your partner throughout your journey together.

Joy in Giving and Receiving:

• The joy of giving and receiving love in a way that truly matters to each person involved is unparalleled. Love language exploration allows you to experience this joy on a deeper level.

Building Lasting Relationships:

• Incorporating love languages into your relationships lays the foundation for lasting and meaningful connections. It contributes to a fulfilling and supportive partnership.

Fun and Creative Expressions:

• Discovering love languages can be a fun and creative process. It opens the door to finding unique and enjoyable ways to express love that resonate with each individual's preferences.

Books:

"The Five Love Languages: How to Express Heartfelt Commitment to Your Mate" by Gary Chapman: The foundational book that introduced the concept of love languages.

"The 5 Love Languages for Men: Tools for Making a Good Relationship Great" by Gary Chapman: Tailored insights into love languages specifically for men.

"The Seven Principles for Making Marriage Work" by John Gottman: Explores key principles for building and maintaining strong relationships.

"Attached: The New Science of Adult Attachment and How It Can Help You Find – and Keep – Love" by Amir Levine and Rachel Heller: Examines adult attachment styles and their impact on relationships.

"Hold Me Tight: Seven Conversations for a Lifetime of Love" by Dr. Sue Johnson: Offers insights into emotional connection and communication in romantic relationships.

Online Assessments:

The Five Love Languages Quiz[1]: Gary Chapman's official website provides a free quiz to discover your primary love language.

Attachment Style Quiz: A quiz to explore your attachment style, which influences how you connect with others.

Websites and Articles:

Gottman Institute[2]: The Gottman Institute offers research-based resources and articles on relationships and marriage.

---

1.   https://www.5lovelanguages.com/

Psychology Today Relationships: Psychology Today's section on relationships covers a wide range of topics from experts in the field.

Podcasts:

"The Love Languages Podcast" by Gary Chapman: Gary Chapman discusses various aspects of love languages in this podcast.

"Where Should We Begin? with Esther Perel": A podcast where therapist Esther Perel provides real, unscripted sessions with couples.

Workshops and Events:

Local Therapy Centers and Relationship Workshops: Check local therapy centers or relationship workshops in your area for in-person or virtual events.

Relationship Conferences: Look for conferences or events focused on relationships, often featuring experts and researchers in the field.

Love Languages:

- The concept introduced by Gary Chapman, refers to the five primary ways individuals express and receive love: Words of Affirmation, Acts of Service, Receiving Gifts, Quality Time, and Physical Touch.

Words of Affirmation:

- Expressing love through verbal affirmations, compliments, and words of encouragement to build up one's partner.

Acts of Service:

- Demonstrating love through actions and services that contribute to the well-being and happiness of a partner.

Receiving Gifts:

- Expressing love through thoughtful and meaningful gifts that symbolize care and consideration.

---

2.   https://www.gottman.com/

Quality Time:

• Prioritizing undivided attention and meaningful time spent together as a way to show love and build emotional connection.

Physical Touch:

• Demonstrating love through physical gestures such as hugs, kisses, cuddling, or other forms of physical intimacy.

Attachment Styles:

• Patterns of relating to others developed in childhood, influencing adult relationships. Common styles include secure, anxious, and avoidant.

Mindfulness:

• The practice of being fully present and engaged in the current moment, fostering awareness and appreciation in relationships.

Polyamory:

• The practice of having multiple consensual romantic or sexual relationships simultaneously, with the knowledge and consent of all involved.

Ethical Non-Monogamy:

• Engaging in consensual non-monogamous relationships with honesty, transparency, and ethical considerations for all partners involved.

Attachment Theory:

• A psychological framework that explores how early attachments to caregivers influence emotional and relational patterns in adulthood.

Interpersonal Communication:

- The exchange of information, feelings, and meaning between individuals, essential for building and maintaining relationships.

Relationship Resilience:

- The ability of a relationship to endure challenges, conflicts, and changes while maintaining a strong connection between partners.

Self-Love:

- A positive regard and appreciation for oneself, emphasizing the importance of personal well-being and self-care.

Intersectionality:

- The recognition and understanding of how various aspects of identity (such as race, gender, sexuality) intersect and influence an individual's experiences.

Attachment Style Quiz:

- A tool or assessment designed to help individuals identify their attachment style, often used in the context of relationships.

Mindful Intimacy:

- Engaging in intimate moments with full awareness and presence, fostering a deeper connection between partners.

Personalized Relationship Models:

- Tailoring the structure and dynamics of a relationship to meet the unique needs and preferences of the individuals involved.

Cultural Sensitivity:

• Being aware and respectful of cultural differences and considering how cultural backgrounds influence relationship dynamics.

Love Language-Centric Lifestyle:

• Prioritizing and incorporating love languages into everyday life and interactions to enhance the quality of relationships.

Disclaimer: The information provided in this conversation, including advice, suggestions, and resources, is for general informational purposes only. It is not intended as professional advice and should not be considered a substitute for consultation with qualified professionals. The user is encouraged to seek the advice of qualified professionals for specific concerns related to their situation.